THOUGHTS ARE THINGS

RUMINATIONS ON LIFE

· REVISED EDITION ·

Luke –
You are
magnificent!

JONATHAN ZENZ

[signature]

ISBN: 978-1983411205

Cover design and cover photograph by Jonathan Zenz
Headshot by Pierre Gautreau

Published by Jonathan Zenz
First Printed 2018
Revised Edition November 2019
Printed by CreateSpace, An Amazon.com Company

www.jonathanzenz.com

For Dane.
You're the FiFi.
Thank you for being my mirror.

How to Use this Book...

This book is a collection of short articles that were written based on my thought process on any given day and are presented here in no particular order except the order in which they were written. Some are my responses to what was happening in the world, some are simply my response to an idea that I hold to be Spiritual Truth.

Each article is meant to stand alone and therefore there is no intention that the book be read from cover to cover in order.

Take a look at the contents... what title appeals to you? Simply go to that article. I am a firm believer that what you need to read will be the article you choose. Let your intuition guide you in the reading.

Enjoy!

Jonathan Zenz

CONTENTS

The "G Word"   1

Simplify   3

Love... Unconditionally   5

Take Your Time   7

Be An Artist   9

What's Next?   11

It's All About You... And All About Them   13

I'm Coming Out – I Want the World to Know   15

Cooperation   17

If You Don't Begin, You Will Never Finish   19

To Be... Or...   21

Be YOU! It's Be-YOU-tiful!   23

Listen, Oh Drop   25

Clap Along...   27

Response-Able   29

A Standing Ovation... Every Time!   31

The Deepest Reflection   33

There's No Time   35

The Fabric   37

Sail On!   39

Curves Ahead   41

The Minority   43

We Know Everything   45

Can't We All Just... (You know the rest)   47

Unfold Your Limitations   49

Exit The Zone   51

Time To Grow   53

Try This...   55

Reconciling Science and Spirituality   57

The Purpose Driven Question   59

There Is So Much More!   61

The Core of All Things   63

Enough With The Stuff!   65

No More Caution   67

To Be Enough   69

Say Thank You For Just One Thing Today   71

What About Tomorrow?   73

Thanks-Living   75

Extended Family is Not So Extended   77

Express Yourself!   79

Be The Beacon   81

Free Your Mind   83

Are You Laughing or Crying?   85

I'm Alive!   87

The Greatest Love   89

Stand Down and Stand Up   91

It's A Matter of Degrees   93

What is Creativity?   95

Speak Up   97

Open Your Understanding by Opening Your Eyes   99

The Fullness of Life   101

It's Natural   103

Be. A Do Nothing   105

God's Plan is Man's Plan   107

Silence   109

Relevance and Response   111

"Thoughts are things, they have the power to objectify themselves; thought lays hold of Causation and forms real Substance. The word of man is the law of his life, under the One Great Law of all Life. Thoughts of sickness can make a man sick, and thoughts of health and perfection can heal him. Thought is the conscious activity of the one thinking, and works as he directs, through Law; and this Law may be consciously set in motion.

Ernest Holmes
Author of The Science of Mind

THE "G WORD"

*If God is infinite—and that is the paradigm
for many faith traditions—then human
beings must be part of God. If we were not
part of God, then God would be finite.*

God.

There it is.

The "G Word."

A word we both worship and fear. And, frankly, it's just a word.

The meaning we ascribe to it is ours to own. We are the ones who decide to live in a place of misunderstanding around the word and what it truly represents. That is what I see to be so prevalent in most discussions of God: misunderstanding.

Let's first consider the language issue. Language is clumsy. It is an effective but sometimes sloppy tool of expression— and it is just that, a tool. So in describing God we have many words and phrases: Universal, Infinite, Loving Presence, Ultimate Creator, the Alpha and Omega, the I Am that I

Am, and on... and on... and on. Yet as we try to explain the ineffable we instantaneously limit it. Any descriptor creates a box and limits that which is unlimited.

It's time we unboxed God.

We have narrowly packed away our understanding of God to make it something manageable in our own mind. In packing it away, we've separated ourselves from the deepest understanding that has been taught by sages and mystics through the ages. We are not separate from this thing called God, we are of God.

"God" is the core answer to the question, "Who are you?"

So this is where I begin. It is my desire to unpack the word God so that we may begin to fear it less, understand it more, and celebrate its true nature.

SIMPLIFY

Are we effective... or merely busy?

What are you doing this week? Are you in the midst of working through the lists of all the things you want to accomplish?

I am a fan of lists and I use them. Yet, I have an objection to lists when the items on them become more important than what is happening in the moment. I have missed out on many great things in the moment because I prioritized another item on a list. I was focused on the things I believed I had to do rather than the things that allow me to feel fulfilled and joyful. From that point of view I began to resent the things I had to do... and that made those things unbearable to complete. Does that sound familiar?

That was the old me, and it can be the old you.

The new me allows flexibility. "Being busy" was stealing my joyful life away and being flexible has given it back.

Now, I am NOT saying to stop doing the things you have to do (although it may be worth exploring who made the decision around that priority—believing we have to do something may mean we've given up choice in our lives, but that's a whole other discussion). We might want to consider a reset to our priorities. If some unique opportunity comes up that you would like to experience... do it. Be flexible and let what you've defined as a pressing item on your list go on the back burner for the moment.

You can always come back to it.

Here's the other thing I've taken into my practice. It goes beyond prioritizing my lists. Eliminate from the list the items that have the lowest priority.

Erase them entirely.

I mean it. Seriously. Erase them. They shouldn't physically appear on the list any longer.

I can hear you asking, "What's the point of that?" and saying, "Those things still need to get done." Even the lowest priority items can chain you into just remaining busy. Eliminating them doesn't mean they wont get done. They will likely end up a higher priority on a future list, in fact you can create a list of "future priorities." Removing the low-priority items entirely makes my list more manageable. I am more effective in my ability to ensure the remaining items are done in a way that ensures quality.

Finally make sure you include on your lists things that you want to do. Add fun items and do them. Your list doesn't have to be all work and no play.

Find the balance.

LOVE... UNCONDITIONALLY

"Even after all this time the Sun never says to the Earth, 'You owe me.' Look what happens with a love like that, it lights up the whole sky!"

-Hafez

Love fully.

Love not because you want anything in return (that's not true love anyway), but simply because you can love. In fact it is actually your natural state of being. So perhaps it is time to give in and become a beacon of loving light like the Sun. There is no reason not to give in to love and fill your personal atmosphere with light!

In my faith tradition I have come to accept a particular definition of love. Love is defined as the creative energy of the universe freely flowing without hindrance. It is the energy that creates, simply because that is its nature—to create.

I know that sounds heady. But just think about what you do when you experience love... you give of yourself freely. At least I am making an assumption that you do based on the fact that when I experience love that is what I do. It seems most natural.

Imagine what might happen if we all decided to daily place our focus on love rather than anything else unlike it. That is a world changing consciousness. When I give of myself unconditionally it is an act of love. If I give and I have expectations or conditions then I live in the possibility of disappointment—which does nothing but make me feel bad.

So give in to your natural state.

Try it out for a while and see what happens!

Simply LOVE!

TAKE YOUR TIME

Two things:
1. Slow down
2. Let go

You know the song, "The 59th Street Bridge Song (Feelin' Groovy)?" The first lyrics are, "Slow down, you move too fast, You got to make the mornin' last." It's great advice. I hear that song playing in my head whenever I feel like I am speeding along at an increasing pace. And I am glad I do, it helps.

Just this morning I've been considering all the things I need to accomplish to be ready for early this afternoon when I am being picked up to head out of town for a retreat. As the things I want to get done before I go pile up I start to feel like I am not going to get it all done. When I feel like that I then start to berate myself in my inner-monologue for not planning better. Then I feel bad about myself... and my the experiences I have become reflective of that mindset. My state of mind literally colors my experiences.

Here are my questions...

Who decided that I had to get all this stuff completed before

I go?

Well... that was me.

Who decided that it was a terrible thing to leave any of it for another time?

Well... that was me.

So I am the only one who is going to suffer any consequence for not getting everything complete. And I am only suffering that consequence because I made a decision to suffer, and it's all in my mind!

Suffering is not a requirement.

I get to make a different choice.

So my choice today is to head to this retreat with a mindset clear of any ill feeling about myself. I get to slow down and let go.

You know what is truly amazing? In slowing down and letting go I am completing my tasks more efficiently.

Go figure.

BE AN ARTIST

Art transforms us at the soul level. Art can transform the world, illuminate the mind, educate the masses, and actively uplift the human experience.

There is something that profoundly connects us all at the level of the heart. We don't realize it, we may not agree with all of its expressions. In fact we may be infuriated by it or fall deeply in love with it. It touches us in every area of our lives whether we know it or not.

Art.

What is art?

A standard definition of art is "works created by human creative skill and imagination." I grabbed that definition from a Google search. I like that definition, because it is open. It doesn't specify fine art, visual art, performance art, commercial art, and the like... but it encompasses all of it.

My mother was a lover of folk art. Our house was filled with folk art, especially the folk art of Mexico and Central America. As an avid traveller she would frequently bring me folk art representations of cats (I now have a great collection). Every piece of art means something. Every piece tells a story.

It means something to the one who created it.

It means something to the one who enjoys it.

The meanings may not be, and frequently are not, the same.

We bring to our experience of art our own history and belief system.

Art has the power to transform our beliefs. It can be challenging, and if we are open, it can deepen our knowledge and enrich the experience of life.

So this is all something that we all may know, or have learned or studied. What it isn't for many of us is a way of life we feel we can be involved in.

Do you consider yourself an artist? If you do, that's wonderful! If not then I offer you an opportunity to change your mind (after all it is your mind... you get to change it if you want).

Deepen into your imagination and see what arises. Then let yourself express it free of judgment. The "free of judgment" is important. Art ultimately isn't created for anyone else—it is created for the artist.

Dare to be an artist.

You can change the world.

WHAT'S NEXT?

Infinite possibilties are present
in this very moment.

I have returned from a weekend at an interfaith retreat and conference center in Santa Barbara, California. I was there with many deeply spiritually minded people for this year's annual retreat. My experience there was lovely, and far too short.

On the opening night of our retreat we gathered in the chapel, I led a guided meditation which was then followed with introductions. It's always fascinating to hear the stories of how people arrived at the place where they now are. While fascinating, these stories are not the defining factor for any of us.

I had to remind myself in that moment to let go of my story. Letting go of my story opens me up to the possibilities which are infinitely available. I think we tend to limit our idea of the possibilities available because we perceive that our life is a singular path that is the result of all that got us to this point. That's not true—only the past is a singular path, the future has no path. It's only in retrospect we see the path we created.

What lies ahead is infinite possibility. Let's not limit that possibility with the erroneous belief that our future is tied to our past.

To move forward is to live the unknown. That's pretty exciting!

Today live in the question, "What's next?" with the intention that anything is possible, because everything is probable

Let your answer to the question of, "What's next?" be magnificent, unexpected, and inspiring!

IT'S ALL ABOUT YOU... AND ALL ABOUT THEM

*Everything in our outer lives is
a reflection of the inner-self.*

One of the difficulties we face in life is based on an erroneous idea that in ingrained in us from a very early age. The erroneous idea is this: other people are concerned with what we are doing and thinking, and we live in a constant state of judgment by others.

It's simply not true.

I find the tendency in my mind to be focused on me, myself, and I. Where did I get the idea that others were thinking about me as much as I think about myself? Doesn't it make sense that if I am predominantly thinking about myself that others are predominantly thinking about themselves?

This came up in discussion last night when I talked about an experience of mine growing up. As a child, when I would tell people about this experience, I would be asked the question, "Wow! Isn't that hard for you?"

"No," was always my reply. I didn't know any different,

so there was no comparison to me about what might be easy or hard in that circumstance of my life. It was a great lesson I learned at a young age. The assumption about the difficulty of my situation arose from these people, because they were reflecting on how they might feel under the same circumstances.

They considered my unusual circumstance through their own lens... so what am I seeing and defining through my lens?

These lenses lead to judgment.

I do work very hard to practice non-judgment. It's not always easy, after all I live in a culture where judgment is the norm. So this method of reminding myself to reflect on the judgments and opinions I have helps me to avoid imposing them on my experience of others.

It doesn't mean I need to keep these feelings to myself if I feel compelled to share them. What it does mean is that I can't expect anyone else to own or process those feelings. They are mine, I own them, and I address them as best I can.

I'm Coming Out –
I Want the World to Know

*Shine your light brightly, it was entrusted to
you specifically so the world could become
brighter by it.*

October 11 each year is National Coming Out Day. It is
a day that was established in 1988 to commemorate the
anniversary of the second March on Washington for Lesbian
and Gay Rights. And, yes, it is about coming out as someone
who identifies as LGBTQ+.

Coming out is not limited to a day.

Coming out is a lifelong process.

I came out in June 1991 as a gay man. I was freshly out of
high school and looking forward to beginning University.
While I was now out, I still had to find my unique identity.
I still didn't know who I was independent of what I thought
society would expect me to be. This was reinforced by the
political activism I became involved with at University.

October 11 was a day when the school group with which
I was associated would erect a freestanding, pink door on

the mall (the strip of grass that ran along most of the length of the campus) and flamboyantly march through proudly stating our "gayness" and encourage others to do the same.

It's taken many years to just be me and live my life according to my own light.

My light is comprised of so much more than an identity of being a gay man. I still celebrate and attend Pride events and involve myself in the LGBTQ+ community, but I don't limit myself anymore.

Coming out is a process of accepting levels of comfort in identity. First one must become comfortable with oneself—if that doesn't happen, then fear will rule. Following that is what many see as coming out—opening up publicly and continuing to live openly.

In my work as a Spiritual Director, I have used the coming out process as a metaphor for how we live our lives spiritually.

First, one must become comfortable with identifying the true nature of being—as Infinite Spirit.

Second, from that place of comfort one may express this publicly.

Third, one can continue to live openly identifying as the Infinite Spirit.

Are you ready and willing to emerge and live life according to your own light without apology?

COOPERATION

"A society grows great when old men plant trees whose shade they know they shall never sit in."

- Greek Proverb

What it is that connects us is far greater than anything that separates us. What strikes me as odd, though, is the degree to which we actively spend energy separating ourselves. Somewhere along the line our culture collectively made a choice that competition had more value than cooperation.

The culture of competition means that someone has to lose to lose for others to feel successful. A culture of cooperation would allow us all to be successful, and to help others achieve success as well.

I believe that there is an infinite Universe. Being infinite there is no end to what it provides for all of us. If we feel limited, it is because we have knowingly or unknowingly allowed ourselves to feel that way. We bought into the feelings of limitation and so we experience it.

To cooperate means we recognize that in an unlimited

Universe there is enough for all of us. We need not fear loss, because there can be no loss.

Let's make choices today that unite us rather than divide us.

Plant the tree because it is rooted in the consciousness of giving. You may not benefit directly from the shade of the tree, but you will benefit in life. That is how the creative nature of love works. Everyone wins.

IF YOU DON'T BEGIN, YOU WILL NEVER FINISH

The greatest minds didn't become great because they had more time than you; that potenial is present in you—with exactly the same time each the day available to you as was available to them.

It all begins with imagination.

When I was a young boy I spent a lot of time by myself. I was an only child until I was ten (there is a whole beautiful story about going from being an only child to having a sister—but that is for another time). Being an only child made me very self-sufficient. I was able to entertain myself by creating from my imagination.

From my imagination I would create elaborate "fantasy-scapes" in the living room. I would conceive of an idea in my mind and try to create the corresponding fantasy world in my mind's eye. I would try to recreate these images from mind. Using strings of lights, bolts of fabric, scores of action figures, and anything else I could find that remotely matched the pictures in my head, I would transform our living room into a fantasy world. It was in the early days of VHS camcorders, and I would video tape these stories. If only those tapes had survived the years.

I am grateful my father didn't discourage my imagination. I am sure it drove him nuts to come home to an apartment in disarray, but as long as I tidied up I wouldn't "get in trouble." So my imagination was allowed to grow. From imagination comes innovation. My imagination wasn't suppressed.

I see in our culture a belief in suppression. Our imagination is easily squashed, giving way to a belief that the important things in life are to make money so that we can be comfortable at some later point in life—that illusive time we call "retirement." Well I don't want to wait. I am ready to to live that life now!

Like the acorn, within each of us is the possibility of the magnificent oak. To grow into the oak, we must dare to break through the outer shell. And we must dare to do it NOW! If we do, we can expect magnificence. If we don't, then we may be supporting others to grow into their magnificence. The only problem with that is, an acorn that is supporting another to grow must be diminishing, decaying to provide nutrients to support others.

There is room for all of us to grow.

It starts with imagination. It develops into innovation.

It starts right now.

Go.

To Be... Or...

"To be yourself in a world that is constantly trying to make you something else is the greatest accomplishment."

- Ralph Waldo Emerson

That is one of my favorite quotes by Emerson. It's pretty profound when you consider the core of it.

We are met with messages at every turn trying to compel us to be something we are not... based on the idea that who we are is not enough. We are not handsome enough, we are not rich enough, we don't wear the right clothes, we don't have the right friends. It's can be infuriating, but also compelling.

Yes, I wrote that it is compelling. I only know that because I see too many of us (myself included) who have fallen into the trap of trying to fit in so that we can be comfortable. That is the compulsion.

Why should we try to fit in?

What makes us amazing is our uniqueness.

So, are you standing out or standing back?

Why not try to stand out today? You have the authority to express yourself in any way you like, not because of what you do but because of who you are. Let what you do become a reflection of who you are!

Be bold!

BE YOU!
IT'S BE-YOU-TIFUL!

We are chained only by what we believe...
we are slaves only to our limited thinking.

What have you bought into that you think you can't break out of?

It's a question I ask myself all the time.

The answer goes two directions, the buy-ins that I want to break out of, and those from which I don't want a break. A lot of my buy-ins work for me, so I don't need to worry too much about them (although it's still good to recognize them for what they are—the result of decisions we've made).

No, the ones that are *not* working for me are the ones I need to break from.

We all need to break from the ideas and beliefs that don't serve us. All those ideas and beliefs do is weigh us down, and work against our natural state of magnificence.

We live in a world, that reinforces many of the self-defeating and self-deprecating thoughts. Yet we should always remember that we have choice, we get to decide the degree to which we live in those thoughts.

I was recently speaking with a student in a class I am teaching about these notions, and where the erroneous ideas, beliefs, and thoughts come from. Much of what we align with in our own minds is the common mental tendency of the groups of people we associate with. We tacitly agree with those predominant thoughts, beliefs, and ideas—and those things become our point of view in how we experience life.

For instance, I pointed out to this student that about ten years ago there was a significant financial slow down in the United States—what many refer to as a recession. Many people were effected by it. Money was lost by many.

Not everyone was effected in this way, though. I was not effected adversely during this time. So, for me it begs the question, "What was the factor that differentiated these groups of people?"

There is only one answer: Consciousness.

The mental decision to participate or not on the part of the individual makes all the difference. It happens at the level of awareness, and below the level of our awareness. That is consciousness.

Don't get caught up in other people's ideas if they are not serving you. That is mental slavery.

We, and we alone, are in charge of our minds.

So… what have you bought into? Do you recognize it?

Good, now you get to choose how to move forward.

LISTEN, OH DROP

"You are not a drop in the ocean,
you are the entire ocean in a drop."

- Rumi

I have woken up this morning feeling a little less than whole. I am experiencing pain from lower back spasms that have rendered me somewhat immobilized. It's not dissimilar to, though not as severe as, back spasms I experienced thirteen months ago. At that time I was left almost completely unable to walk for several weeks.

While I could go to the place of beating myself up and asking myriad questions about how I got to be here, it will only do as much good as looking at the little picture will ever do. Yet that is how we are socialized, to look at the little picture. Look at the symptom and try to fix the symptom. I am much more interested in the big picture. Looking at the big picture is looking to the cause, and addressing the cause.

On today's journey toward the recognition of the cause of my current experience I ask myself the question, "What wants to happen here?" Then I listen... I really listen. I listen to what I hear with my ears, I listen to what I am thinking about what

I hear, and I am listening for that greater intuitive voice. That third form of listening is the really the big picture listening.

I trust what comes up and act accordingly. For me, that is listening from wholeness, and it is in wholeness that I believe I am led to the course of action that heals.

Wholeness heals.

That's always been my experience.

So, off to the doctor I go... with my mind focused on wholeness.

CLAP ALONG...

To be happy is perfectly natural.
Happiness is what you bring to the world,
not what you derive from it.

There is a popular Pharrell Williams song that invites us all to clap along with him if we feel happy. This song led to a recent discussion which culminated in this question:

What is happy?

We know when we feel happy, right?

We know when we feel unhappy.

But what IS happy?

And don't just rely on a dictionary definition. What is happy to you?

When I was posed with the same question, my initial response was, "at ease, free of concern," and as I've ruminated on it that doesn't seem to go deep enough.

I've believed and professed for many years that happiness is not a choice, it is our natural state of being. Experiencing unhappiness is a choice. We don't always make that choice knowingly. Our natural state of being is to be in alignment with the infinite flow... so happy is a flow, it is freedom of choice. Happy is a consciousness.

We don't derive happiness from the things in our lives (although we are taught that we do). We can't create happiness... but we can align with it.

Happiness is the unencumbered flow of creative energy. Only when we block it do we feel unhappy. And boy have we ever learned how to block it, haven't we?

Opening up to our natural state of happiness releases the floodgates of new ideas. From this flows the EXPERIENCE of happiness.

So, "clap along if you feel that happiness is your truth."

Thanks, Pharrell.

RESPONSE-ABLE

Parents can only give us so much, or point us in the right direction. It's up to us to figure out how to be good people.

Do you consider yourself someone steeped in personal responsibility? How do you choose to step-up or show-up in life, especially when a situation arises for which you feel you might be blamed? Is it a practice to say, "Yes, I am responsible?"

Let me clarify quickly, I don't consider personal responsibility the same as blame. Yes, it is one way we define the word, but I came to realize some time ago that to align blame with responsibility was defeating me in moving forward. Blame for any situation bogged me down into the past... what had happened... fantasizing about how it might have been different... and ultimately beating myself up for not having done it better.

How I have come to define personal responsibility now carries with is a forward momentum.

I first consider the situation and the circumstances, whatever they may be. I look at them free of judgment and say:

"I see what has unfolded here."

"I am willing to understand my part in it."

"I own this, and don't need to make anyone else own it to try to make me feel better."

"The journey forward is for me to undertake."

This practice of mine releases blame for myself and others. It opens me up to solutions.

Blame asks, what could I have done?

Responsibility asks, what will I now do?

Moving forward is my personal response-ability.

A Standing Ovation...
Every Time!

The brain is not the mind. The brain is a physical tool for tapping into a Universal and Infinite consciousness. Our individualized use of this consciousness is what we call our mind.

Let's let go of any notion that the mind and the brain are the same thing. The brain is simply the tool we have for accessing consciousness, but it is not consciousness itself. A Broadway theatre—the physical space—does not create Broadway quality productions; it only provides a location. The consciousness of quality preceeds the experience of quality. It all starts in mind.

The physical world is simply a reflection of the Spiritual world. It is very easy for us to align ourselves with the physical expression and forget that it is born of the Spiritual.

What is so important about that?

In the Spiritual all things are possible because Spirit is infinite. I also believe that all things are Spiritual. There is no delineation between the idea in consciousness and the experience in form, except the degree of expression.

Since ALL things are possible, there exists the possibility of discord and disharmony, pain and suffering, as well as blame and victimization. Wow! That's not very inspiring, is it?

Actually, I find it inspiring to remember that if mind can create those negative experiences, then mind can create a polar opposite experience. It is up to us personally to do the work to make that happen if we want ease and grace, wellness and comfort, harmony and peace. That work begins with entertaining ONLY those qualities in mind. The polarities don't go away, but their grip on our mind dissipates.

The ideas that balance on the side of a majority in our mind are the ideas that create our experience in life. Let our minds be like the highest quailty Broadway shows imaginable. The requirements for creating quality theatrical productions require training on the part of all who are involved. So if we want our minds to create the quality life we want we need to train.

Training is the act of actively and consistently focusing your mind on magnificent thoughts irrespective of anything we experience that seems to oppose those thoughts! When we all do that we all triumph and can get the standing ovation we desire!

THE DEEPEST REFLECTION

Everyone, everything, everywhere is the
mirror of my mind and heart.

Reflections of us. They are all around. We are immersed in reflections. We can't escape them. So how do we begin to honor them and learn from them?

A journey to deeper self-knowledge can feel elusive at first. At least it did for me. I mentioned in an earlier part of this book that I was attracted to the faith tradition I now follow because of its intellectual nature. I have since come to know so much more, so much more deeply. It was because I was willing to move beyond the intellect to a deeper place of feeling, and that is where I found the greatest gift life has to offer: True Self Understanding.

That gift is one that keeps on giving, too. We are infinitely deep, there is no "bottom" to self knowledge although we may perceive one.

We frequently offer this idea in educating students in New Thought principles: Do you want to know what's happening in your mind? Look at your life.

We must be willing to take a good look at our life if we want to take steps toward enlightenment (which is not a destination, but an unending journey of deepening). Life is the mirror, reflecting to us all that we have in our mind, and filtered through the lens of our thoughts.

That means all people we encounter are reflections of us. They reflect us in the way they behave around us, in the way they interact with us, and in the intermingling of energetic conscious space we have together. We do the same for them, we reflect them in our behavior, in the way we interact with them, and in the intermingled, energetic conscious space we share.

From these interactions we are constantly making decisions that show up as the effects in our lives. Deepening our self awareness, through observation of the world we are attracting and in which we are interacting can lead to greater expressions of our unique, Divine nature. Provided we do the work.

What do you say? Are you willing to see the world as the mirror to what is in your mind? It may mean there are somethings you will find that you don't like... but you know what is great about that? If you find something you don't like, you are in charge of making the change to better yourself... and the world around you will change too!

THERE'S NO TIME

*Use time wisely. Don't simply fill it with the
work you feel you have to do, incorporate in
your use of time opportunities for play.
That is using time wisely.*

One of the more formidable concepts I've come to appreciate
over the years is this: in the infinite absolute there is no time.
Many times we express this idea by saying, "There is no
time in the mind of God," but what does that really mean?
What are the implications for accepting such a concept?

Well, for me, what it does is allow me to let go of anxiety.
Anxiety is something I experience only when I am projecting
myself into the future. The problem is, the experience of
the future doesn't exist until I experience it, and when I
experience it, it is the present. So the future doesn't exist.

The same goes for regret, which is my re-creating in my
mind the experiences from the past. Those past experiences
no longer exist except to the degree that I hold on to them
and bring them to my present moment. So the past doesn't
exist.

Through anxiety and regret I forget to be in the here and

now.

So if this moment now is the only thing that exists what choices will you make to live this moment as the best moment you can? Living the present moment as best we can is the greatest way to understand the infinite value of time as an experience. Employ it well!

The Fabric

If we took it all away
what would we be left with?
Everything!

Everything we do, everything we say, everything we feel, everything we know is part of an infinite fabric of consciousness. All fabric is interwoven or knit threads.

Let's consider these individual threads akin to our individualized being. Our very being is interwoven with the being-ness of all others. Some of the threads are closer to us than others, but proximity doesn't matter. We are all connected by way of the larger pattern of being, and the fabric stretches out infinitely.

This tapestry wouldn't and couldn't be complete without us. While I (doubtfully) suppose it's possible we could exist without being a part of the whole, I think if that were the case we would not be cohesive or supported by anything. We would just be a loose thread.

That's what it is like to feel alone. We feel like a thread separate from the whole of the fabric of life, and it simply isn't so.

You are an important part of the whole. You contribute to the cohesive nature of the fabric of life, and without you the fabric is made weaker.

Never underestimate the importance of you in this wonderful thing called life. You make the fabric of life stronger, and you are made strong by being a part of the whole.

SAIL ON!

The greatest discoveries have been and always will be made by those who were willing to let go of the known.

Where did we learn that we have to keep a constant eye on what happened in our past as a way of moving into our future?

I am not suggesting that we not learn from past mistakes—clearly we should learn from our mistakes so we don't repeat them—but let's not dwell on those mistakes either.

Have you ever considered that dwelling on your great accomplishments from the past may be holding you back as well? It's true, anything we hold on to will narrow our frame of mind. We limit our own possibility because we narrow the focus of our mind in such a way that we come to believe the future is limited and subject to what we've already created. It's not!

Any limitation we take on in mind becomes the limitation we experience in life.

So…learn from the mistakes, celebrate the great

accomplishments, but remember that those experiences have no bearing on the infinitely magnificent potential you are. So let them all go! They will be there in your memory if you really want to revisit them, but don't let them limit you as you sail on to your next great experience!

CURVES AHEAD

The value of living life is that everything we experience has transformational possibilities. We get to decide.

Are you hard on yourself? Do you find yourself internally beating yourself up for things that you feel you should have done better? Are you willing to rethink that?

I have found freedom! That freedom is in allowing myself to let go of the expectations for a desired outcomes in so many circumstances. Essentially it is allowing myself to straighten out my learning curve.

We all have a learning curve for everything that is new in our lives. Sometimes it feels like we live in a world where the expectation is to bring a depth of knowledge to the table that is not feasible until we've immersed ourselves in the new… and embodied it. So we beat ourselves up. What is the value in beating ourselves up. In my work I am frequently telling people to let themselves off the hook. Isn't it time?

There was a great sketch on the sketch-comedy show "MadTV" some years ago. A patient walks into a psychiatrist's office, the psychiatrist is played by Bob Newhart. In the sketch the doctor tells the patient his billing structure, he charges $5 for the first five minutes and nothing after that—he guarantees that the session will not last the whole five minutes. Why is this? Because following the patient telling the doctor her issue, he gets to the point by telling the patient simply that he is going to tell her two words which she is to listen to very carefully, take them out of the office with her and incorporate them into her life.

Those two words: STOP IT!

Obvoiusly the patient is confused and the humor is played off the erroneous, but commonly accepted idea that we have no control over our mental processes.

We can learn a lot by commiting to stop the mental activity that binds us. To stop it is to let ourselves off the hook. Whatever is happening for you is able to be utilized by you and you have deciding power over how you respond to it.

So make a decision today to straighten out your learning curve, and transform everything in your life's experience to being of value. It's up to you!

THE MINORITY

The majority isn't always right.
Consider the alternative.

Each year in January I visit the Hawaiian Island of Kaua'i to participate in what is known as "The Sacred Journey." It is a special time during which I get to be inspired by wonderful activities and opportunities for deep reflection in one of the most beautiful places on the planet. The journey is a part of the ministry of my dear friends, Revs. Rita Andriello-Feren and Patrick Feren who are the Founding Spiritual Directors of Center for Spiritual Living Kaua'i.

One of the annual highlights of the Sacred Journey is going to visit the Hindu Monastery on the Island. The monastery is home to nineteen monks who live, study and worship there. It is a welcoming place of immense beauty. Each time I go, I learn something new and wonderful.

During my past two visits our group has been honored to have an audience with one of the monks, Paramacharya Sadasivanatha Palaniswami. He lovingly shows us the grounds, and we've been gifted behind the scenes tours of areas not normally open to the public.

During my last visit, as we were visiting one of the behind the scenes areas of the monastery—the room where the monks have meetings and make decisions—the Swami mentioned that part of their process was to make all decisions based on consensus. Without consensus no decision is made and no movement happens until consensus is reached.

Here is the important part of that... it gives the voice to the minority idea in decision making. That voice may otherwise be buried or stifled. It got me thinking about the times I may have pushed a personal agenda without considering the minority voice; there is always wisdom in that minority voice.

We would do well to heed that voice and take its point of view to heart. If it is being expressed, there is something to know in it.

Where are you hearing a minority voice?

Are you able to step back and lovingly consider that voice free of judgment?

Can you really listen with compassion, understanding, and allow the wisdom to touch you at the heart level (and maybe even change your mind)?

We perceive it as a tall task to change our minds—but a change of mind is the activity of potential in motion and a part of the flow of evolution. After all we don't know what we don't know... and what we don't know may be reflected in that minority voice.

WE KNOW EVERYTHING

At the end of what is known is the beginning of the deeper sense of the infinite.

What do you think you know?

It's a loaded question.

Personally I think I know a lot. I have learned a lot from books, from observation, from delving into the relative information available all around me. In fact, upon first meeting someone whom I've come to know as a sister, I famously uttered the phrase, "I know everything," and it's become a bit of a joke between us. That utterance was about a particular conversation that I had overheard—but, fundamentally, to know everything is also a Spiritual Truth.

The Spiritual Truth is this: We have access to the infinite breadth of knowledge of the Universe. However, we've been socialized in a way as to not tap in or trust the infinite. When we *do* tap in... we call it intuition.

We also may be missing the information we seek because we are limiting our way of receiving it. We limit our access by qualifying the value of the information all around us. We decide whether the information is good or bad, helpful or not. Just like the minority voice I have also written about, there is something important for us to consider in everything that we hear. As my mentor in ministry has frequently reminded me, "God is speaking no matter who is talking." So the less we judge what we are hearing, the more we open ourselves to learning and knowing.

The expression of our innate intuition shows up everywhere. Let's not limit ourselves to what we already think we know and open up to the unlimited possibilities of infinite knowledge and wisdom. We have unlimited access to actively know more and more, and it is up to us to keep searching and questioning and allowing ourselves to be open to the answers (whether we like them or not).

We actually DO know everything, because we are the living expression of the infinite.

We are one *of* God, and God knows everything.

CAN'T WE ALL JUST...
(YOU KNOW THE REST)

When we remember who we are we cannot help but know that truth for everyone around us. To know we are of God is the great equalizer. We cannot condemn anyone else when we know who we are and who they are.

One of the daily practices I've taken to heart, because I used to take things so personally, is to live by this motto:

Don't confuse a difference of opinion with a personal condemnation.

I see so much divisiveness in the world, and there seems to be no end to the degree to which we can seem divided and act out based on that frame of mind. It's sad really, and sometimes I feel it's out of my control. I feel helpless, and resigned to experience a life that is limited to the little petty things "out there."

What I realize is this, I cannot feel helpless and resigned unless I am not tending to a deeper understanding of life. That deeper understanding of life is the unfolding cooperation of the infinite by means of creation.

What does that mean? Well, when I take the time to look more closely at what is all around me I can see harmony, and a natural world in balance. What that tells me is that *balance is the natural state of life*. I connect more deeply with the core of my being, which is *of* God. There is no separation from me and the rest of the balance in nature, unless I allow it.

So I must rethink my habit (and it is a habit) to condemn those who disagree with me. I don't need to take it personally and I don't need to react by launching personal attacks.

It's a practice. I practice this every day, because I am faced with differences of opinion everyday. There is room for all of it. I step out of my own way and trust in the flow.

So what do I do about all I see in the world that seems out of my control? Well, I trust that I am a beacon and an example of what can be: civility, compassion, and cooperation. It begins with me. I must be those things if I expect to experience them in my world.

Unfold Your Limitations

Our only limitation is ourselves.
We are inherently abundant and unlimited.
When we allow an opening to this truth
the flow is unstoppable.

Expanded awareness is a great gift we have in this thing called life.

Are we using it wisely?

Are we using it well?

There is a school of thought which suggests that the human experience is the highest level of expressed consciousness on this planet because we have the capacity for self-awareness. I don't know if that it true. I sometimes look at my cats and it seems that they have some level of self-awareness. So I ask, "What is it that sets me apart from them?" There are two answers I've reflected on over the years.

The first is that we have expanded awareness—awareness of that which is *beyond* our personal and limited idea of life. I don't know that my cats have that awareness. That idea is pretty esoteric for this moment.

Perhaps the more widely understandable idea is this: we have the capacity to be self-reflective. In being self-reflective we can modify our behavior. This is something I don't necessarily see in my cats. We might be able to temporarily curb their behavior, their response is related more to a change in stimulus from the outside. I can spray them with water when they do something I would prefer they not... but the change in behavior is not because they've reflected on why they are being sprayed with water, only that they don't want to be sprayed.

We don't need to be sprayed with water, because we have the ability to reflect on our behavior, make determinations about it, and act accordingly.

This begs the same questions I began with:

Are we using this awareness wisely? Are we using it well?

Only we can know for ourselves. No-one else can tell us.

In your expanded awareness, allow yourself the chance to self-reflect and set the compass for your own ethical standards based on what you know to be inherently true—my question for reflection is usually, "Is this loving and kind?"

You get to live according to your paradigm, and I suggest being open to flexibility within this as well. Don't become so set in your ways that another idea, based on new information, around which you have exercised self-reflection, cannot then modify your moral compass. That is how we expand and grow. It is also a way we can open our hearts to more compassion. Self-reflection can be a tool in deeper understanding and experience of others.

EXIT THE ZONE

*We easily live in our comfort zones and are
ultimately trapped by our comfort zones.*

I think one of the scariest things we experience in life is
facing the unknown. At least we think it's scary. And in
thinking it is scary, we experience the fear.

I am a personal fan of encouraging people to push the limits
of their comfort zone; and yet there are things I wouldn't face
myself. Life sure is a balancing act. In my mind the things
I *won't* face feel extreme. For instance—I won't try bungee
jumping, or skydiving, or anything else where there is some
form of free fall. I don't like the idea of a floor being taken
out from under me. At the same time, I absolutely adore zip-
lining (at least I still feel the connection to the line which is
supporting me).

But it's not just about the physical limits in our lives—what
are the mental blocks we've placed on ourselves that we are
unwilling to push past? Do we feel a lack of support, like
we might go into free fall without a parachute, by giving our
mind over to the unknown?

Perhaps.

Here's the kicker: Absolutely everything that is in front of us is unknown. We might think we have an idea of what we will face, but we don't. I don't really know what is going to happen thirty seconds from now, let alone thirty days or thirty years.

We've convinced ourselves that we have limits, but those limits hold us back, and those limits are only in our minds. I used to have a limitation of thinking that I was shy (notwithstanding people's experiences with me—I am frequently considered by others quite gregarious). When I would go to a party, I would stand in the corner hoping someone would talk to me; but I couldn't possibly make the effort myself because it was too risky to face the possibility of being rejected. Rejection, to me, was like the parachute not opening.

It actually took a lot for me to move past that fear—and I still face it occasionally—but I am glad I did move past it when I did. It was because I stepped out past the comfort zone and said, "hello," that I met the man who is now my husband.

I couldn't possibly have known in that moment what the next thirty seconds would hold, neither could I have known that three years after that we would be married.

In retrospect I see it. It makes me wonder what other opportunities I've missed because I hid behind my own fears.

What fears do you need to face today?

TIME TO GROW

Press against the wall, don't let the concept
of brick and mortar hold you back. That
resistance and pressure may be the very thing
we need in order to grow strong and evolve.

I was recently reminded of something that came up for me a couple years ago in a conversation with a friend who was experiencing a challenging issue in his life. He had come to me for spiritual guidance and this idea was a result. He felt like everything around him was falling apart. I said to him,

"When the experiences in your life begin to unravel it is because your greatness can no longer be contained by the limitations you've put in place. God cannot be contained, so something new must be born."

Holy smokes. That landed with him. And I am glad it did.

To be honest, it landed with me! And still does!

There is a natural flow of life that sometimes means we must be willing to let go of that which no longer works. We can do this gracefully, or we can fight it. How we react becomes the experience. At the time, knowing that an unraveling in life was a press for perfect evolution through me was a hard pill to swallow. Finding the place and way to embody this idea has made my experience of life much more grace filled.

I don't fight with evolutionary unfoldment any more. If I find myself in the fight—I ask myself, "What self-imposed limitation am I fighting like hell to hold on to... and is it really in my best interest?" The majority of the time I conclude that holding on to the limitation is most definitely NOT in my best interest.

Yet, letting go can be hard. We spent time to create the limitation, we feel it as a part of us. We've come to define ourselves based on the limitations we've created. So letting a limitation go is letting go of a personal defining factor. When we move through this we go through a grieving process.

Allow evolution, and take care of yourself through it. It may mean that you need to grieve.

Know that there are people like me who are here to support you when you need it.

You are not alone.

TRY THIS...

"All life is an experiment. The more experiments you make, the better."

Ralph Waldo Emerson

There is a word we use that is thousands of years old. It is older than the English language (which is my point of reference, American english being my primary language). In all the time it has existed, the word has had almost no change in meaning. The word spans religions (specifically Abrahamic religions) and cultures. It occurs to me that most people likely don't really know what it means unless they've taken the time to look it up.

Amen.

It is a ubiquitous statement at the end of a prayer, it signifies that the prayer is complete. But what does it really mean? Etymologically the word originates in Hebrew. The word simply means "truth," and is used adverbially as a way of confirming something to be so. Basically, to say amen is to say, "and so it is."

In my faith tradition, Religious Science, we say the same

thing at the culmination of a prayer, we just use the English to say it.

And so it is.

There is a great power in making that definite statement. Saying, "and so it is," or, "amen," means there is no other acceptable option. This is the power of our word which is how our lives show up. And we are doing it all the time, whether we say amen or not.

The words we utter are the results of thoughts we have… those thoughts are rooted in beliefs which are the cornerstones of creation. Do you truly believe what you are saying? Or is what you are saying subconsciously in opposition to your core belief? Which is stronger?

I know what I believe.

Here is a test to try, at the end of everything you say throughout the day, follow it with, "and so it is." In that moment, check in—do you truly believe it? Listen to that small voice in the back of your mind, it will be there to reflect to you the truth only you can know. After all, I can say something with the appearance of conviction, but that doesn't mean I believe it. True conviction comes from within. So test the waters. See if what you say matches with the belief by uttering, "and so it is," or, "amen," at the end of your statement.

If the belief doesn't match what you would like to experience in life then begin the mental work to strengthen a new belief and allow the grip of the old dissipate.

That's how we change our lives.

Reconciling Science and Spirituality

Know your mind. Feel your heart.
Know your heart. Feel your mind.

One of the first questions I was asked by my mother when I told her that I had become involved in a spiritual center (specifically telling her that I had started attending a Religious Science center) was, "You can still go to the doctor, right?"

It is a common misconception about Religious Science (besides being mistaken for Scientology) that we don't utilize standard medical care. It couldn't be further from the truth. We go to the doctor, we take medication, we engage in the benefit of all that Spirit has to offer—because it's ALL Spirit, or God. It is actually a misstep to believe that we shouldn't seek out medical care and indicative of a limit in mind that suggests that medical care is somehow not Spiritual. I like to say, "God is in the pill."

The care we seek is accompanied by thoughtful and heartfelt prayer in support of healing. It also doesn't negate the idea that we *can* heal using the power of mind only... and I trust that I am led to the right path and the right tools to accommodate that healing.

Ernest Holmes, the founder of Religious Science, was very clear:

> *"We believe in medicine, surgery, psychiatry, and psychology; we believe in anything and everything that aids. Our system of thinking excludes nothing; it is all-inclusive."*

Transcribed from the "Seminar Lectures"

This comes up for me as I am hearing of the various medical diagnoses of multiple people in my life. There is power in the work of medicine.

And you must know what is right for you. What sets your mind to a place where you can focus on healing? That wisdom comes from the heart, and must be felt deeply to be effective. After all, our experience of life comes in degrees. The greater degree to which we believe in perfect health, that is the degree to which we will experience perfect health. If you believe medicine will help, then it is an aid to the mind and heart. If you believe that medicine won't help, then it may be a hinderance to healing. It is all in truly getting clear on what you know to be true in your heart.

So, here is to heart health!

Here is to clarity and wisdom.

Spirituality and science go hand in hand, after all they are both the result of the same Universal Mind.

THE PURPOSE DRIVEN QUESTION

What is yours to do? Do it!
The world needs your greatness
to shine brightly forth.

What is in your heart to do? Have you given in to that deep-seated desire?

Wait, before you answer, let's get clear on one thing: this is not really about the "what" but about the "why." What do you think is the "why" around the desire in your heart—and is that "why" strong enough to actively motivate you toward the fulfillment of that desire?

This is all tied in to your PURPOSE—is your purpose driving your life or are you being driven by "what." I have worked with many people who can clearly articulate their "what," but are less able to clarify their "why."

They live life with these ideas as primary:

"WHAT I should do... WHAT I should be."

How is it that we've come to place so much focus on the

"what" as opposed to the "why?"

What is about how you are perceived by others. If your main motivation is "what" then you might be living based on someone else's idea of your purpose. In being able to articulate "why" you live your own purpose. To live your "why" means you have the self-esteem, self-respect, and self-reliance to lead a purpose driven life, unencumbered by other's opinions and judgments.

If all humanity gave in to only living the "what" then we wouldn't progress and evolve. It is only those who push against the bounds of societal pressure, peer pressure, family pressure who have taken us to the next level.

So what is in your heart to do, and more importantly, why is it in your heart to do?

Clarify your "why" in all things, and the things that are most evolutionary for you will reveal themselves. You may find you want to let go of some things in your life. Have the willingness to do so. You will free up your life to more fully invest in the "why."

Let your greatness shine forth! Light the way! Give us more to see!

You are magnificent!

THERE IS SO MUCH MORE!

"There are more things in heaven and earth...
Than are dreamt of in your philosophy."

William Shakespeare
(Hamlet, Act 1 Scene 5)

Are you excited about life and learning? I am. I am a seeker and always looking to know more today than I did yesterday. There is power in being able to consider more than we think we know.

The whole concept of philosophy, as we know it now, is primarily defined as the study of reality and existence. I have found myself in adherence to the philosophy of Dr. Ernest Holmes called "The Science of Mind and Spirit." It works for me because it feels practical, yet flexible and evolutionary.

The core idea of philosophy can actually be found in the root of the word itself—at its root the word means, "the love of wisdom." I like that.

Let's fall in love with wisdom. There is so much more to know about the nature of life and the Universe. It is a great joy, to me, to be able to explore it. I don't want to take anything for granted. So how do we explore it?

Ask questions and do not take answers as gospel. In some ways it is like reverting to being two-years old again and incessantly asking the question, "Why?"

The more we explore the nature of everything that exists, the more we can know about ourselves and our place within it. But, let's not only look to the outside. Let's explore and come to know more about what is within too. For the depths of wisdom are unlimited, they are beyond time and space. The more we look "out there," the deeper we see. The more we look "in here," the deeper we see. It works in both directions.

We are boundless and unlimited—so let's go deeper.

Ask more questions. Get excited!

THE CORE OF ALL THINGS

"No one speaks of creating energy, but only of transforming one form of energy into another."

Thomas Troward

Everything is energy. Everything is either potential or kinetic. We experience and interact with energy in myriad ways. Ways we are aware of—and ways of which we are not aware. From heat… to magnetic… to light… to sound… to chemical… to gravitational… and more… EVERYTHING is energy and everything is interacting as energy.

Energy acts upon energy.

Energy can be manipulated and harnessed.

Since we are energy… we can act upon energy. We can manipulate and harness energy.

This is a rudimentary way of getting to the bottom of this idea: we are in TOTAL control.

We are energy and so is everything we experience, and everything with with which we interact. So we must have some effect on the energy all around us. Shall we harness it and use it to our advantage?

Spirit is energy. Matter is energy. It's all the same.

Perhaps I am being too esoteric today... but my goal in this is to get us all to think more deeply about our fundamental nature and the connection we have with the fundamental nature of the whole.

After all... it's all the same thing.

ENOUGH WITH THE STUFF!

How do we begin to let go
when it means so much?
How do we process change
when we deeply feel comfort
in the space the heaviness makes?

If we hold on to the lead
our hands are not open to receive the gold.
Truth lies in our hands and our heart.
Break it open now.
Let go.

One of my favorite songs these days is a great tune by Brendan James called, "Simplify." It calls for each of us to take stock of the things we hold in our lives and the things that surround us. Basically… it asks us to question things… and simplify our lives.

I've had the opportunity to simplify in my life, and at times the opportunity to simplify came to me in an unexpected (and not very nice) way. When I was in my mid-twenties I was in a challenging relationship. When I decided to end the relationship, I left the apartment we were living in together, literally walked out, and I stayed away for a week. Upon returning I walked into a completely empty apartment.

Completely empty.

It took me by surprise in the moment, yet as I had time to reflect, I realized that I ended the relationship with my self-respect in tact, and he left the relationship with a lot of stuff.

Stuff is just stuff. If you lost all your stuff today, would you be able to hold your head high or would you feel defeated or destroyed?

Perhaps its time to let go of the mental hold we have on stuff.

Simplify.

No More Caution

> *"One, alone, in consciousness with the*
> *Infinite, constitutes a complete majority."*
>
> *Ernest Holmes*

I've just completed a virtual call with a group of Spiritual Leaders from across the continent and today's topic of conversation was "growth." I had an interesting experience with the directive from our group leader. We were asked to let go and turn our attention to the inner world and allow a visualization to come to mind... the image created would represent "growth."

Nothing... and I mean absolutely nothing came to mind for me.

It took me by surprise in the moment, because I tend to be a visually oriented person. Then I realized — that "nothing" was the blank canvas that has been laid out before me. There is a tremendous feeling of freedom that comes with that! I was called upon to reflect upon my vision for growth, unencumbered by circumstances.

When it comes down to it, we must let go of the cautious

living that has developed only as a result of limitation in thinking. When we accept some fact as truth, we limit our future potential until we break that connection.

So this is what it is to release into Oneness.

There is support for your vision out there. Find it! Let go of any circumstance or notion that limits your vision and give in. If we ALL give in to vision, then the world of experience becomes transformed.

TO BE ENOUGH

> *"I searched for God, and found only myself. I searched for myself, and found only God."*
>
> *Sufi Proverb*

When will we get it that we are enough?

We may not feel like we are enough. That is only because we succumb to societal pressure to be more, to give in to the rat-race, to achieve... and achieve... and achieve!

I have a secret—you will never be more that you are in this moment right now.

Before you get down on yourself (or upset with me for suggesting such a thing) let me clarify… when we take away all the self-judgment and live outside our perception of what others think of us, what is left? When we let go of the façade of doing, what is left? When we look deep within our soul, what do we find?

We find that there is only an interconnected wholeness. We are each of us individualizing the whole—and in being individualizations of the whole we can never be more than we are, because the whole is Infinite. Nothing is more whole than whole.

So let go of any sense of limitation—you are unlimited wholeness.

Let go of lack—you are abundant wholeness.

Let go of disease—you are the wholeness of pure health.

Let go of loneliness—you are the Infinite Love of the whole.

If we live each day with this as our understanding, we might approach the experience of life differently.

I'll stake my very existence on it.

You are enough. You are! I promise!

SAY THANK YOU FOR JUST ONE THING TODAY

"I am grateful for what I am and have.
My thanksgiving is perpetual."

Henry David Thoreau

I know you've heard it. You will be more successful if you live in gratitude. We are encouraged to keep gratitude journals and go to bed with gratitude on our minds, but what if it feels overwhelming?

Do you ever find yourself feeling like you have nothing to be grateful for?

Have you struggled to get that gratitude list done?

Does it feel like you SHOULD be grateful for something because it is expected? Do you ever beat yourself up for "should-ing?"

Don't kid yourself. Allow yourself to really experience gratitude. It should a practice, not a chore. So how do we begin practice gratitude in a way that is experiential? Start with this, let yourself off the hook if you don't feel it yet.

You can't force it. Start with one thing. Right now, in this moment, let go of any thought of what should be, allow yourself the luxury to relax and ask yourself the question, "What am I grateful for right now?" Then allow an answer to come to you.

Allow. Don't force.

Simply let it be.

The answer may not be what you would expect.

Let yourself feel it no matter what it is!

That is how gratitude begins!

Day one!

WHAT ABOUT TOMORROW?

"If we make every day a day of praise and
thanksgiving, a day in which we recognize
the Divine Bounty and the Eternal Goodness,
and if we live today as though God were the
only Presence and the only Power there is, we
would not have to worry about tomorrow."

Ernest Holmes

So many of us are worried about tomorrow. Yet we seem to forget that tomorrow will be the result of what we have in mind today. If we are ready to make change we must not procrastinate. Do it now!

Gratitude is a great practice for changing all our tomorrows. And it goes hand in hand with forgiveness. Can we each find forgiveness in our heart and allow ourselves to be full with gratitude too?

I have been working on a project for the past week and a half—it has been a challenging experience. The challenge has run more deeply only when I find myself in a place of blame for what has been. That is totally counter-productive and makes me miserable, me and no one else. So what I have done is to go to gratitude for the ability to do the work and forgiveness for any belief that I have that may be blameful of the work to begin with.

You know what? The experience (while taking much longer than I expected) has been one of joy. If I bring joy in my heart to the experience, the experience ends up being joyful.

We should consider that in all we do. Joy is not derived from experiences—we bring the joy to the experience.

So don't put off gratitude and forgiveness until tomorrow! If you delve into them today you will experience joy today, tomorrow, and forever more!

THANKS-LIVING

Be here now.

Be grateful now.

It's the only time we have.

What you don't know is what can hold you back from the fullness of gratitude. I suggest we fully give in to gratitude right now. I often say this is the only moment that exists, and I was reminded of that again today.

I was faced with the news of the passing of a friend today. It was unexpected and sudden and under circumstances most people would consider tragic. Being among most people—I can affirm the tragic nature of the circumstances that lead to this untimely death. No more detail is necessary for my point… when I heard of his passing I wondered if there was any place in my heart where I hadn't lived in gratitude for the part he played in my life.

Gratefully, there wasn't.

What if there had been?

I won't spend time to consider the alternatives—but I will look to recognize if there is any place where I still need to go to gratitude. Is there anyone with whom I feel at odds? Can I let it go and replace that with gratitude? It will lead to better relationships and a more fulfilling experience of life. I guarantee it!

What I don't know is whether I will even be here tomorrow. So there is the urgency for beginning in gratitude. This is the only moment, right now.

I am grateful.

EXTENDED FAMILY IS NOT SO EXTENDED

My family tree has deep roots, short branches,
and many, many beautiful blossoms.

I have discovered that I have more cousins that I once thought. While there are genetic markers which will prove scientifically that I have connections about which I am currently unaware (but finding out all the time), the more meaningful familial relationships to me are those people with whom I share my life. Whether they be friends, genetic relatives, or in-laws, everyone is my family. The people I don't know all around are actually my family as well. So it is no surprise any longer when I find out about genetic connections.

We are a small band of over seven-billion on this small stone in the Universe. Actually in the scale of the Universe we don't even inhabit a stone—more like a microscopic fraction of a small grain of sand. Each of us, at the fundamental core of our being, is totally connected—we are formed of the same "stuff." It is literally true that each of us elementally are comprised stardust. On the atomic level, all that we are is a reorganization of the elements created when stars exploded.

Not only does that connect us all, it connects us to the whole of the Universe. We are that immense!

So I live in gratitude for all my family—those whom I know and those whom I have yet to meet.

I let go of my judgment, disillusionment, upset, annoyance, and anger and allow it to be replaced with gratitude and thanksgiving. In doing so, I find myself back in the metaphorical garden where my alignment is more attuned with connection to the whole rather than separation. Let's all go back there.

We are that we are.

I am that I am.

You are my family.

I will meet you in the garden of star stuff.

EXPRESS YOURSELF!

Live by gratitude. Let it echo in every word
you say and be reflected in every thing you
do. That is true Thanksgiving.

In so much of my Spiritual work there is talk and work to cultivate a of feeling gratitude within, and that is very powerful, but what about expressing gratitude outwardly? We should be open about our feelings of gratitude. When I was growing up the practice of writing thank you notes was very prevalent. Now, with the advent of e-communications, that practice seems to have fallen by the wayside. It's sad to me.

If I want change it's up to me. So today I personally commit myself to being much better about writing notes of gratitude, and sending them via the mail service. A handwritten note is so nice to receive, isn't it?

I don't need to have received a gift to express my gratitude, either. I can send notes unexpectedly to people in my life for whom I have gratitude in my heart. The person to whom I write may have no idea of the impact they've had in my life—so why not let them know. It makes me feel great, it makes them feel great, and joy abounds!

Express gratitude! You (and everyone you thank) will be glad you did! We, collectively, can make the world a much better place. Let's start today with this one thing!

I am grateful to you!

BE THE BEACON

Illuminate the dark shadows
of discontent with your love.
Shine your light as a wayshower.

What would happen if you didn't let ANYTHING get to you? I mean ANYTHING AT ALL! To approach the world without negative emotional responses or buttons being pushed is a tall order. Yet, we all can be in control of our responses to things and circumstances all around us.

It's not that things won't happen.

Things do happen.

It is not entirely about how we respond, it is about how we lead in consciousness and love to become a beacon to others. If we can maintain our place as a consistent and infinitely loving presence in the world, we become the living example of compassion. We don't have to agree with everything, and we get to express our opinions—but a loving approach is to learn to express those opinions in a way that does not make other people "wrong" for the opinions they hold. In a world that is increasingly polarized that can feel like a tall order. It's not impossible, however, and if we begin to act in accordance with that ideal we encourage others to do the same.

So how do we begin?

Take a breath. In that moment of breath let yourself move, in mind, past the *instinctual* response you may have to differing opinions. Let your mind process the information before responding. Ask yourself, "Does this truly require my response?" You might find your response is not necessary. If that is the case—don't respond.

If a response is warranted, then let your next consideration be this: "Is what I am about to say being said in a loving and compassionate way?" or "Is what I am about to say only being said in an effort to make another person wrong?" Consider speaking only from the former and not the latter. After all, how would you like to hear the information being offered?

If we begin by tempering our responses, speaking only from love, and allowing the light to prevail, we will quickly change the tone of public discourse. Let us each be the beacon of light to address the darkness. Let us each be the beacon of love to address any hate.

That's how we change the world.

Free Your Mind

My unencumbered freedom, my independence, is my joy. Nothing can catch me in a trap when I embrace True freedom. It is my birthright.

We must not allow ourselves to be blind. One of the greatest challenges we face in our lives is admitting we don't know something. We are faced each day with navigating and negotiating the unknown (and everything ahead of us is totally unknown—even when we think it isn't). We do our best to make educated guesses to determine courses of action in life; most of the time those guesses are spot on. We have developed the capacity to make those guesses based on a lifetime of embodying habits of thought. Much of our mental response to the world is habitual.

If we are willing we can observe those habitual responses and question them to great benefit. Let's begin to question those responses, beginning with answering the basic question, "Is this line of habitual thinking serving me in a constructive way?" Since these habitual responses are based on past experience and past development of thought, it might be worth getting to the root cause of the thought. What was it in our history that convinced us so thoroughly that our habit in thought was the right answer? Is that reasoning still valid?

Many other people, experiences, and events have shaped the individuals we have become today. Our alignment with these things will continue to shape our experiences until we actively decide to embody something else. We mustn't be afraid to look at these things. We must look beyond the narrative to the deeper aspects of how the narrative has shaped our life. From this place of understanding—the work begins.

Work daily to uncover these habits. As you do, make decisions about them. Keep in mind, though, that these habits are not good or bad when you really recognize them—*they just are.* Honor them for being the roots grounding you and growing you to the place where you are today. Learn from them, and then either accept them as habits you would like to continue or release them to embody new habits.

This level of work and mindful awareness can change your life. It doesn't happen in an instant, but persistence pays off in the long run. Keep up the great work of deepening awareness and developing constructive life habits!

You are worth it!

ARE YOU LAUGHING
OR CRYING?

*"Life is a comedy or a tragedy
and you get to decide."*

Ernest Holmes

I've been doing research into my family history lately. I was inspired by an aunt who had one of those mail-in DNA tests available. She offered it to me and so I took it. Before I received the results I started looking more deeply at my historical roots, this got me thinking about the decisions my ancestors made. It begged the question for me, "What are the consequences of our choices?"

Choice is a great factor in the expression of our spirituality. The capacity to discern through reasoning is truly a feature that sets us apart from other species. What we do with that discernment shapes our lives.

We can shape our lives. Actively.

That's big.

We are not subject to anything "out there."

We get to make of our lives what we want.

We may get stuck in thinking that some event that has occurred has bearing on our lives. It only does to the degree that we allow it to. We get to make choices about our point of view—and our point of view colors the experience.

I come from a background in theatre, and I learned early on that the only difference between a comedy and a tragedy is the point of view. The same script can be used, in most cases, to create a comedy or a tragedy depending on the point of view of the director and actors. I have had scripts I've written as comedies be directed and performed as tragedies and that is how they are experienced by the audience (much to my chagrin).

What is the approach you are taking to the script of your life? Are the choices you make being made from the point of view that life is a comedy or a tragedy? Simply something to ponder!

I'M ALIVE!

Come alive.
You were meant to experience the fullness of
life and give of yourself in a way that affirms,
"I am an experience of infinite joy!"
Do it for you and no one else.

I love to experience life. Life is meant to be lived deeply, freely, and fully. For a long time, though, I thought I had to "be something to the world" in order for my life to have value and meaning. I was mistaken in my idea that how I was perceived by others was the measure by which my value should be based. That paradigm kept my experience of life at bay—because, if what I wanted to experience didn't fit within the paradigm, I would disregard it, avoid it, and do "what was right."

That made life pretty blah.

It made me a pretty blah person.

Who wants that?

I have come to know that no one wants that!!

We think that's what people want, yet when I truly consider the options I find myself more excited to have self-reliant people in my life than to have sycophants who are only trying to please others.

So what do you need?

What do you want?

What makes you come alive?

THE GREATEST LOVE

The greatest love of course is the love of self.
When we love ourselves we cannot help but
share that love with the world.
We need self-love more than ever.

In a seemingly cynical society it seems trite to say it these days, but it is a fundamental truth. Loving yourself is the greatest love of all.

I grew up a teen in the nineteen-eighties. The recording of "The Greatest Love of All" sung by Whitney Houston got a lot of air play during my teen years (I was twelve when it was released). It struck a chord with me, even though I didn't really give much thought to what the lyric of the song was saying—yet to this day I know every word in that song without a second thought.

How many of us are really living up to the standard of true self-love? Is there any way we are undercutting our self-love? Why do we do that? More important than understanding why—can we let go of anything that keeps us from self-love and delve deeply into the truth of love?

Loving yourself must become a habit, not just lovely lyrics

in a song.

Love is creation. Love is infinite. Love is "givingness."

When we give of ourselves, to ourselves, we lift ourselves, and have so much to offer the world.

It is up to us to love ourselves unconditionally.

I see only love.

I hear only love.

I feel only love.

I express only love.

And every moment I freely live in love.

I am love.*

   *And so are you!

Let's go forth and live love accordingly.

Stand Down and Stand Up

"What other people think of you is none of your business."

Attributed to many different people including Deepak Chopra, Wayne Dyer, Regina Brett, and RuPaul

I have a love/hate relationship with social media. I love to look and see what people post (and take a lot of it with a grain of salt). I hate when people use it as an excuse to simply be mean. I read an off-putting comment recently on a photo post. The photo was beautiful and celebratory and uplifting.

The comment suggested that the person who posted the photograph had isolated themselves from the "real world" and work that had to be done to make our world better.

This exchange got me thinking, what business is it of anyone's how we show up and express in the world?

The truth is, the commenter is entitled to their own opinion. However, I believe we should keep our opinions to ourselves unless they encourage positive action (not shame anyone into submission).

So—as the quote says, "what other people think of you is none of your business." Conversely, "what we think of other people is none of their business." So we might do well to keep it to ourselves.

If we can't keep it to ourselves, let's find a way of engaging in civility and respect. Spoken communication is fifty percent what is said, and fifty percent what is heard—when we tend to our fifty percent, as a speaker, from the point of view of unconditional love it makes the receptor, well, more receptive!

The other part of the truth about the previously mentioned social media post, is this: the photograph doesn't indicate that the poster is isolated from the real world, and the real work. I happen to know the person who posted the photograph very well—and it is someone who is deeply understanding of and active in the work to be done to make this a world that works for everyone.

I don't think any of us intends to be mean, yet the social media world has skewed our sense of compassion a little. At least the comment I read came from someone who didn't hide behind an alias.

Let's work together to make the world a better place—compassion and civility are were we can start ourselves. When we show up in that manner we can expect the same returned. If we are faced with something else—we are the ones in charge of our reaction to it. I suggest we act from love and not take any of it personally.

I start today by standing up as LOVE!

It's A Matter of Degrees

*Blood is thicker than water, but not as thick
as respect and joy derived from true familial
connections—even when those connections
are with members of our chosen families.*

I am back to considering my genetic history and ancestry
today. It's challenging to trace all the intricacies of family
dynamics—especially since there are aspects of life that
may go unrecorded. For instance, my paternal-grandfather
was adopted. I know about that fact in the line. Because I
know that he was adopted, I also have been able to identify
his birth parents, and link back from that. I know about that
genetic connection.

A genetic test can tell us a little bit. Research can tell us a
little bit more.

At the end of the day maybe the best thing we can discover
is that we are all related in the grand scheme of life. It's true,
isn't it? If we go back far enough into the history of life (and
I am talking about more than a finite human experience) we
are all part of the same infinite wholeness.

Let's take it back even more to before there was life on this planet. If the matter of the Universe has always existed, and everything is comprised of various incarnations of that matter, then we've all become the living, breathing accumulation of the Universal matter that has always existed.

I happen to be the accumulation of matter known as me—but every atom in my body has existed in some fashion for as long as the Universe has existed. So I am at least thirteen-billion years old. While the sum of my parts in this incarnation of experience is only a few decades old, the parts themselves are as old at time itself.

What does it matter? Well, when we begin to truly get past the limited ideas of separation and realize we are truly of the same stuff, perhaps discontent and discord will cease to be a part of our expression and experience. Let's approach each other with love, respect, and joy—full in the knowledge that at our core we are all related.

Let's create a global family. We can do it!

WHAT IS CREATIVITY?

Creativity and imagination,
while related, are not the same thing.
Creativity is imagination activated.

Do you nurture your creative self? Do you actively engage in creative work?

Creativity is the capacity to see below the level of the obvious, and to use what we find to bring something new into being. To be creative is to allow a balance of intellect and intuition to flourish.

We often align creativity with artistry. When compared to our "everyday work lives," (doing what has been deemed by culture and society as "important") we may consider artistry something frivolous. It's not. Study after study has shown that those who have greater access and practice in the arts produce better results in the workplace. To remove artistry is a tragedy for our society. Those who have delved into artistry more easily allow creativity in every other area of their lives.

So what is it to create? To create is to bring something into being. To see possibility where none may have been seen before—and then allowing that possibility to evolve itself in form. Nurturing and encouraging the creative nature within allows us to broaden our perspective in all aspects of our lives.

The truth is we are all creative—we are creating all the time. Are we, however, limited in our focus of creative solutions or are we broad in the possibility?

By nurturing creativity through artistic endeavors we broaden the possibility of ingenious solutions to infinite problems. We don't have to be Mozart, or Rembrandt, or even Lady Gaga—all of whom were or are possibly artistic geniuses. They certainly didn't have an issue with letting their creative artistry flow. We don't need to be them; our work is to simply be ourselves. Be the best artist and creator you can be. Encourage the creative nature within by delving deeply into artistic endeavors.

When we do this life becomes a more beautiful experience for all of us. We deepen our awareness of what is really important: connection and cooperation.

So begin to look below the level of the obvious. What is there? Let that something within come to the surface and bless the world with. You are the conduit for that something so don't block it!

SPEAK UP

Democracy is more than elections.
It is the exercise of making our voice heard.

The worst feeling in the world to me is the feeling of helplessness. I can't stand it. When I feel out of control of my life and my circumstances—that's the time to reconnect in spiritual practice.

If my life is created in my mind then I get to re-create my life when I feel out of control. I get to change the experience by changing my mind.

This has been at the forefront of my mind today because of all that is happening in the world of U.S. politics. It's very easy to sit back and feel like there is nothing that can be done, but that's not the case. The best thing we can do is speak up. Let our voice be heard. That's a great deal of democracy. If I decide not to speak up about something, then I've decided to give up my power to change what I want changed.

Active participation in democracy as a constituent doesn't mean that I should have to protest to have my voice heard. In representative government we must contact our representatives—both for the things we don't support and for the things we do support.

When we speak, a great spiritual practice is to ensure we speak from a heart-centered point of view rather than from a reactive and emotional state. We are certain to be heard and understood more readily when we do this.

There are ways of ensuring that the position from which we speak is a position of love, respect, and compassion. Although the political scene doesn't seem to be representing those attributes very often these days, we can be the point at which change unfolds for the better. So in voicing our opinion be loving, respectful, and compassionate—and also be clear.

Activate your life by participating in life. Fear not! Your authentic voice has value. Using it adds to the great conversation and eliminates the feeling of helplessness. Speak up! You'll be grateful you did!

OPEN YOUR UNDERSTANDING BY OPENING YOUR EYES

Believeing is seeing, not the other way around. Our eyes are the lens taking in the information which is then decoded by mind and heart. The mind does the seeing, really, and all our seeing is tinted with the color of our beliefs felt through the heart. So a red door isn't just a red door—it's our feeling about a red door that makes it something.

The more we look the more we see that everything we experience is simply a veil. There is some animating force back of it all. We are exactly the same as that animating force—and we are NOT our bodies, we are the energy and activation behind our bodies. We are NOT our experiences, we are the driving force behind our experiences.

Why this is important is because it demonstrates a fundamental (yet often challenging to grasp) truth that we are completely in control of our experience. It's easy to get lost in the idea that we are not in control.

Can you deepen into that belief?

What comes up for you that challenges that idea?

Are you able to look through that challenging thought to a more mystical understanding of the truth?

When we know we are in complete control of our experience, because we are in the process of evolving through the experience at all times (there is never a time when we are not in the process) then life can get better. It gets better because we make a deeply rooted decision to allow it to be better.

There is a story about how I came into being in this philosophy that is telling. I first found myself in a spiritual center that was also a theatre. I was involved in a production at that theatre and during the run of the show I was invited to go to a Sunday Celebration to meet someone as a potential love connection (yes, it was a blind set-up).

I resisted because I was not in the frame of mind that supported the idea of being involved in a spiritual community. I was VERY resistant.

After a while, I thought, "well, one Sunday isn't going to kill me." So I went.

I did find a love connection—me.

I had to make the shift in mind to be able to be open to it.

I had to deepen my understanding. I had to open my eyes.

My life has become more expansive and joyful because I allowed myself to be open to the fundamental Truth of being: I AM.

The Fullness of Life

"It is not enough to be busy. So are the ants.
The question is: What are we busy about?"

Henry David Thoreau

I avoid saying I am busy.

Frequently when I want to get a point across around what there is, or has been, to do in my life that has occupied inordinate amounts of my time I will say, "I am experiencing a full life!" And that is the truth, but am I giving lip-service to what is behind the statement? Just changing the words to support a more "spiritual" understanding doesn't change the intention, if behind the statement is the belief that my life is, "busy."

I do engage in a lot. I keep myself very well occupied.

Here's the question that comes up for me today: What am I giving up to maintain that pace?

This past weekend I had a lot of fullness to experience (i.e. I was VERY busy). This fullness kept me from completing some things that I enjoy.

It's very frustrating to me to feel like I don't have time (which is an illusion and only the case when I make time a priority). What if I didn't make time a factor—would I still accomplish what I want to accomplish? The real answer is, "I don't know." I don't know because I have been living in the habit of prioritizing time and filling up my available hours in the day for so long I don't really know if I can function free of the consideration of time. Theoretically I know I can—but frequently theory and practice do not meet.

So my life is definitely full!

I think it is time for me to accept a slightly more fluid relationship with time. So here is where it begins.

IT'S NATURAL

*"That which today seems to us supernatural,
after it is thoroughly understood, will be
found spontaneously natural."*

Ernest Holmes

I frequently can be found contemplating the concept of Laws and Principles in our universe. What I seem to come back to is that ultimately all laws are the same. The Laws and Principles of the Universe are all expressions of the Divine Law of Cause and Effect.

Take, for instance, gravitation. It is spontaneously natural; we don't give it a second thought. But what is it? Basically, in layman's terms, gravitation is the agency that attracts objects with mass to one another. So—everything with form has an attraction to all other things with form. Gravitation is the thing that holds the entire Universe together. It is a demonstration of the law of attraction in our physical world.

We can't see it, but we know the effects of it. To date we cannot measure the actual essence of gravitation, but we can measure its effects. Gravitation is always at work, it always has been regardless of our cerebral understanding of it.

Like gravitation, the Divine Law of Cause and Effect is always at work. We can measure the effects of the Law as things unfold in our lives based on our thoughts and beliefs, but the actual essence of it is hidden from our eyes. We know it and we use it always regardless of our awareness of it. It is natural. To many it may seem supernatural, as though we use the Law as though it were magic to create demonstrations in our lives.

God is not magic.

God is spontaneous.

God is natural.

BE. A DO NOTHING

Do. Be. Do. Be. Do?
Be. Do. Be. Do Be!

"What can I get?"

"How do I create more?"

"How do I fix my life?"

"What is wrong with me that I don't get this stuff?"

You can attract everything you require.

There is no "how" in creation.

There is nothing that needs fixing—recognize that.

Simply, there is nothing wrong with you.

It is certainly true of me, and I suspect many others, that when we were first learning about the metaphysical philosophies of New Thought teachings, there was an immediate reaction of human ego that suggested that we are the ones who were creating. We work very hard to make change in our lives and when things go awry we begin to believe that "this 'stuff' is a lot of mumbo jumbo."

Our recognition of this is only from the relative and limited viewpoint grounded in the mechanics of being, focused on the "stuff" of life, rather than the life behind all stuff. It is with continued practice that we come to realize that there is nothing that we create in our lives.

Do you think you have the ability to create? If you answer "yes" (provided that "yes" is rooted in the limited belief that you are separate from God) you are wrong. God is the creative power of our lives. We have the ability to attract the highest good to us through daily spiritual practice; but we do not create—God creates through us, as us.

Our spiritual practice brings us to the understanding that we are one "*of* the infinite power" we call God.

We do not need to create in our lives. If we seek to express God only, and recognize God in all things, then perfect expression happens.

Do less. Be more.

GOD'S PLAN IS MAN'S PLAN

> *"So God created man in His own image; in the image of God He created him; male and female He created them."*

> *Genesis 1:27*

Does God have a plan? Does God want something for me? To suppose that God has plans and desires for me is to imbue God with human characteristics. How can this be? God is the Allness of the Universe. Isn't it limiting to anthropomorphize God? If God is unlimited... then God is unlimited. There are no degrees of "un-limitation."

God doesn't decide for me whether I am healthy or sick, rich or poor, with whom I have relationships in my life, and God doesn't decide what I do for a living. Right?

Wrong. God does decide. God decides through me, AS me—because I am OF God. I am a conduit of infinity and experiencing God's life as my own. I am but one conduit among infinite conduits. I say this not to limit myself, or to undermine the limitless expression of God. The decision of God is MY decision. When I decide to be healthy—I am healthy. When I decide to be rich—I am rich. When I decide to have friends—I have friends. When I decide on perfect creative expression it happens perfectly.

God doesn't care what my expression is because it can't care. If I stop getting in the way and allow God to express, then the perfection of the infinite follows suit—I am healthy, rich in money and relationships, and I have the perfect job. That is what God wants for me—because that is what I want for myself. That is what feels right. If I feel limitation it is for me to confront and correct.

It is our use of consciousness that governs our experience. This is where we have the gift of making a decision that is cemented in an unfailing Law. Anthropomorphizing God AS ME is ultimate freedom because there are limitless possibilities in my life and I am only limited if that is where my belief is rooted.

God's plan is my plan.

God's desires are my desires.

SILENCE

Listen.

I have made a career of breaking the silence. My life as a minister is to speak—and teach—and spread the message I have to spread through whatever means are made available to me. Basically, my job is to make noise.

Noise isn't always necessary, however, and frequently noise is the last thing we need to find our way to a deeper sense of connection. I frequently engage in the practice of silence (and I am certain that might surprise the majority of people who experience me in an un-silent way). Silence allows me to deepen into my practice of understanding. Silence allows me to listen.

Listening is a great habit to embody.

I have often found discord begins where listening ends.

So today the message is simple.

Allow silence…

~

~

~

~

~

~

~

~

~

~

~

~

~

~

~

~

And so it is.

RELEVANCE AND RESPONSE

Who is God really?

Is God that separate all knowing presensce from the Bible who felt compelled to constantly involve himself in the affairs of human-kind and then seemingly disappeared entirely from involvement?

I realize the answer now: Of course not.

God is us.

In a world of constantly growing expression and connectivity do we feel we have to control it all? If so, do we have to do it alone? If this is our point of view I am here to remind us all that it is not the Truth. Rather it is a misunderstanding of the human experience. We have become infinitely engrossed in the minutiae of the world of form in which we have our conscious awareness and expression—we're constantly working more and more, harder and harder, thinking and believing that we have to control it all.

This mental misfire is not something that seems to have been required or needed for people of faith. The players in the Bible, from those who set down the scriptures to those about whom the stories were told, all had the Faith *of* God. The faith of our society seems to have shifted to the worship of consumerism. We live in the faith that there will be food and clothing available in stores, that the water will run from our faucets and that whatever mess we make will be cleaned up by someone else. We have let go of responsibility and connectedness not only to something beyond ourselves but to our fellow man. We have forgotten about the Unity of the Universe.

I believe, once we return to the understanding that we are not only surrounded by "the unseen," but a part of it then the world will transform. Religion will truly be irrelevant when we return to the understanding of Oneness.

> *"Why are some healed through prayer while some others are not?... The answer is NOT that God has responded to some more than others, but that some have responded to God more than others."*
>
> *- Ernest Holmes, The Science of Mind*

Stay open to hearing God through you... for it is that voice in the back of your mind.

Stay open to seeing God as you... for God is what you see reflected in the mirror.

Respond to God, by being of God.

Acknowledgements

I want to thank all my spiritual teachers, but primarily I have to thank Dr. James Mellon. In 2004 I met this man who would forever change my life. There are no mistakes in this world, and when I first walked into the NoHo Arts Center for New Thought on that beautiful winter day my path was changed in a profound way.

I want to thank my family, and specifically my father, Don, who offers the greatest, unconditional support a son could have. He has encouraged me to stretch beyond what I thought I could be. That encouragement has allowed me to expand into the unparalled experience of magnificence in my life.

My greatest gratitude is reserved for my husband, Dane. He puts up with my Spiritual habit beautifully and has become one of my greatest teachers. Thank you, Dane, for reminding me of the path when I forget. I will love you always.

Made in the USA
Lexington, KY
16 November 2019